Rembrandt

Rembrandt

JESSICA HODGE

PRC

This edition published by
PRC Publishing Limited
The Chrysalis Building
Bramley Road, London W10 6SP
An imprint of **Chrysalis** Books Group plc

ISBN 1 85648 622 2

Printed and bound in China

PAGE 1: *Self-Portrait with Saskia,* 1634, British Museum, London.

PAGE 2: *Flora,* 1635, The National Gallery, London.

Contents and List of Plates

Introduction

Rembrandt is undoubtedly the greatest Dutch artist of all time, one of the unparalleled masters of the European tradition. The roots of his work can be traced in that of various predecessors, but his growing mastery of technique was subordinated to an increasingly personal view of what his art should address, which at times left him out of sympathy with his contemporaries. His range was immense, comprising history painting, portraits, landscape, genre paintings and self-portraits, and his work has been regularly criticized by those who feel that its very variety betrays the lack of a clear theoretical viewpoint. One contemporary writer described him as the 'first heretic in art.' A further complication is provided by the fact that he had many pupils throughout his long life, which has created a problem of attribution. Since 1968 the Rembrandt Research Project, based in the Netherlands, has been engaged on the task of identifying which 'Rembrandts' are genuinely by the hand of the master and which are the products of his studio. The result has not been without controversy.

Historical Background

When Rembrandt was born, in Leiden in 1606, a new nation was in the process of establishing itself, both politically and geographically. The area we know today as the Netherlands had had a checkered history. United by Charlemagne, it had been divided again under his successors into small sovereign feudal states. In 1516 the Netherlands came under Spanish rule, when Duke Charles inherited the Spanish throne through his mother Joanna, daughter of Ferdinand of Aragon and Isabella of Castile. Ironically, Spain itself had only been united in 1479 when Ferdinand, having led his wife's successful campaign for the throne of Castile, inherited Aragon from his father. In 1519 Charles also inherited the crown of Germany from his maternal grandfather, the Holy Roman Emperor Maximilian l, and was himself crowned Holy Roman Emperor as Charles V in 1520, thus becoming by far the most powerful monarch in Europe.

The Spanish administered the Netherlands as part of a huge global empire that included substantial possessions in the Americas as well as Europe. Dutch resentment of foreign domination and economic exploitation was reinforced by religious differences. The European Reformation, which had ostensibly begun in 1519 with the revolt of Martin Luther against the teachings of the Catholic Church, led to the establishment of Protestantism in large parts of northern Europe, including Switzerland. Much of the inspiration both for the Revolt of the Netherlands and for the French Wars of Religion in fact came from the Geneva Protestantism of the French reformer Jean Calvin, rather than from Lutheranism. The teachings of Calvinism were more readily intelligible and systematic, its synodal organization more appealing to secular leaders, than the inspired individualism of Lutheranism or its more radical rivals.

BELOW: Nicolaes Visscher's *Map of the United Provinces* of 1667 shows north at right, and is framed by twelve views of the main cities of the Republic.

ABOVE: Johannes Lengelbach, *The Dam at Amsterdam with the New Town Hall under Construction*, 1656. Rembrandt's painting *The Conspiracy of Claudius Civilis* (page 102) hung in the Town Hall briefly in 1661-62.

In the mid-sixteenth century, opposition to Spanish rule in the Netherlands was united under William 'the Silent', German count of Nassau and prince of Orange in France (1533–84), who inherited vast possessions in the Netherlands, and at first tried unsuccessfully to unite all seventeen provinces. In 1579, however, seven of the northern provinces, including Holland, Zeeland and Utrecht, joined as the United Provinces in a pact of mutual assistance, the Union of Utrecht, which was to form the basis for the Dutch Republic. William of Orange-Nassau and his successors became the 'first servants of the Republic,' with the title of 'Stadholder' or governor. While the southern provinces, including Flanders, remained subject to Spain, with a governor and an ostentatious court in Brussels, the northern provinces renounced the rule of the Spanish king Philip ll in 1581.

The ensuing war lasted sporadically until 1648, with the Dutch establishing considerable maritime power, particularly after England's defeat of the Spanish Armada in 1588. By blockading the mouth of the River Scheldt, the Dutch closed the sea access of the southern city of Antwerp, and instead Amsterdam in Holland took on a new role as a dominant trading center, not only for the immediate coastal regions, but for much of northern Europe. During the 1590s the Dutch economy blossomed, based on Baltic trade and herring fishing, and the foundation of the Dutch East India Company in 1602 offered spectacular opportunities to increase the prosperity of the infant Republic. A series of maritime defeats persuaded Philip ll of Spain to agree a Twelve Years' Truce in 1609, three years after Rembrandt was born, which effectively recognized the United Provinces as a sovereign state, permitting the consolidation of both economic and political power. Independence from Spain was only finally confirmed by the Treaty of Münster in 1648, but the second stage of the struggle, from 1621 to 1648, formed part of the broader European conflict known as the Thirty Years' War. Little of the fighting took place within the United Provinces themselves, and the growing merchant class continued to enrich themselves and their country.

In addition to the establishment of a political identity, the period 1550–1650 also saw dramatic changes in the landscape of the Netherlands. With much of their agricultural land lying below sea level and protected from flood only by a complex system of dykes, the Dutch were at the constant mercy of the North Sea. From the 1560s flooding became increasingly severe, and in 1570 a storm swept aside the North Sea defenses along the whole length of the coast from Flanders to Denmark. The two battles, against natural forces and human invader, became inextricably linked in the national consciousness, and the rebel leaders were occasionally reduced to using the one as a weapon against the other, notably in the relief of Leiden, Rembrandt's home town. Besieged by the Spanish in 1574, and with Haarlem already fallen, the defenders of Leiden were succumbing to starvation and disease when William of Orange-Nassau made the decision to breach the dykes and flood central Holland. Combined with a September storm that made the waters deep enough for a rebel flotilla to sail almost to the city walls, this bold move saved Leiden. The story became part of a national epic of deliverance by sea, wind and the guiding hand of a Protestant God which played a significant part in the culture of seventeenth-century Holland. William of Orange-Nassau referred to 'an unshakeable union' with God that clearly superseded any allegiance to an earthly sovereign (but particularly a foreign, Catholic one), and the sense of being a chosen people appears constantly in the Old Testament themes of much Dutch painting, including that of Rembrandt's early maturity.

Individual landowners had already been active in land drainage in the sixteenth century, but the invention of the wind-driven water-pumping mill, and massive capital investment, vastly accelerated the pace in the early seventeenth century. In the area north of Amsterdam, cultivatable acreage had increased by 40 per cent by 1640, transforming the domestic economy of northern Holland and making it possible to feed the exploding population of Amsterdam. Much of the work was funded by syndicates of urban capitalists; the Beemster drainage project produced a return of 17 per cent for its 123 investors.

Although each of the provinces that constituted the Republic retained a measure of political individuality, they were linked by the States General, an assembly mainly concerned with joint foreign policy, and by acknowledgment of the position of the Stadholders, descendants of William of Orange-Nassau, who held the title of captain-general of the union and continued to provide military leadership. In religious terms, Protestantism in various forms dominated, but almost uniquely in Europe at this time, both Catholicism and Judaism were tolerated. The resulting freedom of worship attracted many immigrants, reinforcing the cosmopolitan nature of a society already globally connected though its commercial interests.

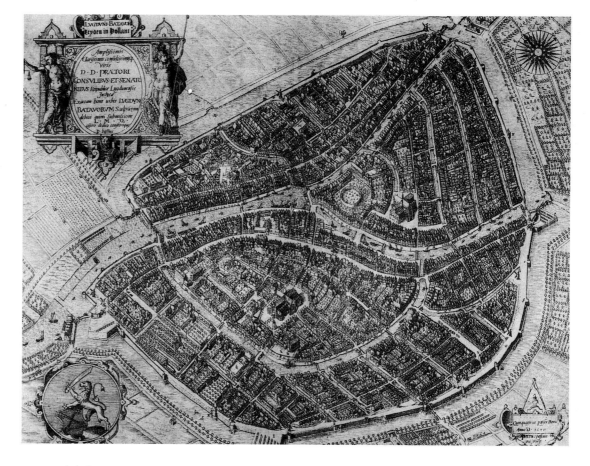

Dutch Art in the Early Seventeenth Century

The truce of 1609 marked the final political separation of the Northern from the Spanish Netherlands. The latter remained an aristocratic society, with artistic patronage in the hands of the court and the principal landowners. Flemish painting of the early seventeenth century is represented above all by the Baroque style of Peter Paul Rubens (1577–1640), who learnt his trade during a prolonged visit to Italy, 1600–09, and introduced a heroic scale and a mastery of historical narrative into the hitherto intimate world of Flemish art. History painting included not only scenes representing actual historical events, but also legendary, literary or, above all, religious incidents, treated in a suitably noble and edifying way, and was generally regarded as the highest branch of art until well into the nineteenth century. The Catholic Rubens's success in Antwerp was established with his two huge triptychs for the cathedral, the *Raising of the Cross* and the *Descent from the Cross* (1610–14), which showed his mastery of this field.

The new Dutch nation, on the other hand, was distinguished from the rest of Europe by its democratic constitution and its Calvinist religion; the latter had important consequences for the arts. Calvinism allowed no decoration in churches, so there was no call for magnificent altarpieces or sumptuous religious furniture, and the political climate was hostile to overt display by the richer or more powerful citizens. On the other hand, Calvinism released the artist from the rigid iconographical tradition imposed by the Catholic Church, and per-

mitted a far more immediate reading of the Gospels, a freedom of which Rembrandt made full use. Despite growing prosperity, however, largescale commissioned works of art were rare in the Republic. Dutch architecture was sober, classical and restrained. Jakob van Campen's Mauritshuis at The Hague (1633–44) is small and domestic by grandiose contemporary standards; the grander City Hall of Amsterdam, designed after the 1648 treaty as a monument to the prosperity and power of the new country, still shows the same restraint and lack of ornament. The new society was essentially urban and middle class, and this gave rise to a clearly definable and flourishing native school of painters, concentrating on smallscale work and realistic subject-matter and recording every aspect of the world around them. They excelled in landscape, still life, portraiture, genre scenes, animal and marine painting. They tended to specialize in a particular subject; Frans Hals (c.1580–1666) worked almost exclusively as a portrait painter, while Jan Vermeer van Delft (1632–75) took genre painting to unparalleled heights, but was barely recognized by his contemporaries. This was not an art of dominant individuals; Rembrandt remained uncharacteristic, and his work did not dictate the development of painting as did that of Rubens in the southern provinces.

The Republic provided a lively market for native art. The English diarist John Evelyn, who visited Rotterdam in 1641, reported that:

. . . Tis an ordinary thing to find a common farmer lay out two or three thousand pounds

in this commodity (i.e. paintings); their houses are full of them, and they sell them at their kermesses (fairs) to very great advantage.

The majority of pictures were produced for an open market, and if an artist did not please that market, as was the case with Vermeer, and with Rembrandt himself in his later years, they were reduced to an extremely precarious existence. In that sense the art market in the Republic was much more akin to that of the twentieth century than to other European countries in the seventeenth century; the Dutch artist offered his wares to a mercantile society, unsupported by any form of patronage, whereas elsewhere the artist continued to have a subordinate, but guarranteed, social function, in a princely and ecclesiastical society with a great appetite for the visual arts as a form of power statement. The Stadholders did exercise some patronage – Rembrandt himself received a substantial commission from Prince Frederick Henry in the 1630s – but on a much reduced scale, and commissions also came from individuals and civic bodies, principally for portraiture in its various forms.

Rembrandt's Early Years

Rembrandt Harmenszoon van Rijn was born on 15 July 1606 in Leiden, an elegant and prosperous center of the cloth industry, situated south-west of Amsterdam on a branch of the Rhine. The family connection with Leiden is documented as early as 1513, when Rembrandt's great-great-grandfather is mentioned as a miller there. Milling, a lucrative business in a still largely agricultural community,

LEFT: Peter Bast's *Map of Leiden* shows the city in 1600, shortly before Rembrandt's birth.

BELOW: Johannes Vermeer's *The Art of Painting*, *c.*1666, focuses on the painter and his subject, whereas Rembrandt's *The Artist in his Studio*, *c.*1629, is dominated by a painting.

remained the family occupation; Harmens van Rijn, as the joint owner of a mill, belonged to the moneyed middle classes, and Rembrandt's oldest brother Adriaen followed the same trade. Rembrandt was the ninth of ten children, but by the time his mother died in 1640 it seems that only four survived, as her quite considerable estate was divided between Rembrandt, his brothers Adriaen and Willem and his sister Lysbeth.

It seems that Rembrandt stood out as unusually gifted from an early age, and was sent to the Latin School in Leiden. His parents apparently destined him for the university in Leiden, and it is possible that he began his studies there, but he had soon persuaded his family that

painting was his chosen profession, and by 1619/20 he was apprenticed to a respected local painter, Jakob van Swanenburgh (1571–1638). The Catholic Swanenburgh is now known chiefly for his apocalyptic visions of hell, and it is difficult to isolate any elements in Rembrandt's early work which might be attributable to Swanenburgh's influence, but presumably he gave his pupil a thorough technical grounding.

To complete his training, Rembrandt was sent to Amsterdam, to the established history painter Pieter Lastman (1583–1633), who played a rather more significant part in the young painter's development. Lastman spent most of his career in his native Amsterdam, but between about 1603 and 1607 he was in Italy, where he seems to have come under the influence of Caravaggio's dramatic lighting effects and naturalistic approach to history painting, and also of Adam Elsheimer's bright colors and animated, crowded compositions. On his return home, Lastman specialized in religious, historical and mythological scenes, but his approach to history painting was rather different from that of his predecessors. His principal interest was in conveying the actual structure of the

story in a clear narrative, rather than simply presenting a virtuoso artistic performance. In his *Odysseus and Nausicaa*, for example, the composition is carefully designed to present the clearest possible account of events. This stress on adherence to the text relates closely to Dutch realism, but realism in turn militated against history painting; the contemporary instinct was for the known and familiar, rather than for flights of mythological fancy.

In choosing Lastman as his master, therefore, Rembrandt was already setting his face against the current trend, which was toward specialization and away from largescale narrative. No work of his is known from the six-month period he spent with Lastman, but the first securely attributed painting by Rembrandt after his return to Leiden in 1625 to set up his own studio, *The Stoning of Saint Stephen* (1625), falls clearly into the category of largescale narrative. Adam Elsheimer had painted the same subject some 20 years earlier, and although there is no evidence that Rembrandt could have seen the work (Elsheimer worked in Italy from 1598 onward), the dramatic lighting, rich colors and busy composition all recall the earlier artist.

A much more personal touch is the first known self-portrait by Rembrandt, the appalled face which appears just above the saint's head, and it has been suggested that the artist also modeled the stone thrower and the saint on his own likeness. This is the first in a long and unparalleled series of self-portraits that reappears at intervals throughout Rembrandt's life. Few other painters have so consistently questioned the nature of their own likeness, both as visual autobiography and as part of an enduring interest in narrative, and the self-portraits remain one of Rembrandt's greatest achievements.

BELOW: Rembrandt's first teacher, Swanenburgh, specialized in nocturnal occult scenes, such as this painting of *The Sibyl Showing Aeneas the Underworld.*

RIGHT: *Christ on the Cross*, 1616, by Peter Lastman, who was the leading history painter in Amsterdam when Rembrandt was apprenticed to him, and proved a far more substantial influence on the young artist.

The bulk of Rembrandt's work in Leiden – he stayed for another six years in his home town before moving back to Amsterdam – was devoted to figure subjects, and the impression given by these early works is of an artist experimenting with and finding his feet in several different spheres at once. The development was rapid; only a year after the somewhat tentative *Saint Stephen*, he painted a much more confident, coherent and harmonious scene, again on a religious theme. This time the subject was drawn from the Apocrypha, a section of the Old Testament often included as an appendix, but not acknowledged as part of the Hebrew canon and not printed as part of the Protestant Bible. The *Book of Tobit* concerns a dedicated servant of the Lord who continues to serve his faith despite the prohibitions of the rulers of Israel, and despite his own encroaching blindness. His wife Anna earns a meager wage spinning, and one day comes home with a kid, a gift from one of her employers. Hearing the kid bleating, Tobit assumes that it has been stolen, and rebukes his wife. Anna in turn grows angry and reproaches her husband for his readiness to suspect others. Rembrandt, as he was so often to do, focuses on the moment of revelation, as Anna forcefully states her case and Tobit realizes that he has been unjust. The colors are restrained, the figures dominant, the drama immediate,

but in later representations Rembrandt was to discard much of the detail which he finds necessary here. The narrative influence of Lastman lingers in the spindle, which tells us how Anna supports herself and her husband, the string of onions, the bird cage, the basket, the shelf of domestic clutter, which all add to the verisimilitude of the scene and reflect the contemporary obsession with realistic detail, and yet in the end detract from the drama of the story. In later work, Rembrandt pared detail down to a minimum and focused on the protagonists and their reactions; here the expressive precision of elderly hands and faces anticipates one of the mature Rembrandt's most enduring strengths.

Scenes from both the Old and New Testaments provided themes for Rembrandt throughout his career, some of them familiar subjects, such as Christ's Passion, some of them more unusual, such as *The Rich Man from the Parable* (1627). Here an old man surrounded by account books counts his wealth in a darkened room, shading with his hand the candle flame which harshly illuminates his face from below. This stress on chiaroscuro (contrasting effects of light and shade) to highlight the narrative, is reminiscent of the work of Caravaggio and becomes particularly characteristic of Rembrandt's work during the 1630s, when his painting was at its most flam-

boyant and theatrical. In the roughly contemporary *Christ at Emmaus* (c.1628), a single light source is again used to dramatic narrative effect, with the figure of Christ silhouetted in such a way that he appears to the viewer to be the source of the light.

By 1628 Rembrandt was sufficiently well established to take in his first pupils, one of whom, Gerrit Dou (1613–75), stayed in Leiden when Rembrandt moved to Amsterdam. Dou became one of the most successful and fashionable artists of his time, founding the Leiden school of 'fine painters', whose meticulous technique has its roots in the detailed precision of some of Rembrandt's early works. Taking in pupils was standard practise for an acknowledged master, probably also a financial necessity, and the normal means by which novices acquired their artistic training. In Amsterdam, Rembrandt achieved enormous popularity as a teacher; one of his biographers describes how he 'filled his house in Amsterdam with almost countless distinguished children for instruction and learning.' Even toward the end of his life, when his work no longer commanded so much admiration, he seems always to have had pupils, but as his painting became more restrained and personal in the 1640s and 1650s, it also became increasingly difficult to follow. His later pupils adopted

11

his motifs, types of composition or arrangement of colors, but in a haphazard and eclectic fashion which misses the subtlety and spiritual insight of Rembrandt's later work.

If Rembrandt lost no time in establishing the pattern of his career as a teacher, the same is true of his painting, and most of the themes and qualities which characterize his mature work are present in embryo in the Leiden paintings. The earliest independent self-portraits date from 1628–30, and show Rembrandt experimenting with different techniques and lighting arrangements. Self-portraits, although not unknown in seventeenth-century Dutch painting, were usually treated as an opportunity for artists to display themselves as respectable members of society; Rembrandt's exploration of his own appearance, in unposed renderings without embellishment, are unique. The *Self-Portrait* of 1628 yet again uses the light source in a novel fashion, with the artist shown three-quarter face but largely in shadow, and only his right cheek and hair clearly illuminated. A similar work painted a year later is both smoother in technique and much more formal in mood, and is more typical of the type of public persona an artist might be expected to project.

Another strand in Rembrandt's early work which is traceable throughout his career is the poignant depiction of old age, both in narrative painting, as already noted with reference to *Tobit and Anna with the Kid*, and as single-figure studies. Early examples of the latter are sometimes tentatively identified as Rembrandt's parents, and it is certainly tempting to read in these sympathetic and dignified depictions some reflection of a harmonious household, although the paucity of the sources allows no such speculation. As with the self-portraits, however, it is perfectly possible that a young and impecunious artist would use the models he had to hand. One of the most appealing of these has been tentatively entitled *An Old Woman: 'The Artist's Mother,'* (*c.*1629), which was in the collection of Charles l of England as early as 1633, an indication of the young Rembrandt's early success. The same model appears in other depictions of elderly women at this time, notably *The Prophetess Anna* (1631), in which the richly dressed subject studies a page of the Scriptures, from which the light reflects back onto her face. Perhaps the culmination of these early studies of old age, and a companion to *The Prophetess Anna*, is *Jeremiah Lamenting the Destruction of Jerusalem* (1630), with its meticulous rendering of extreme old age in the balding, wrinkled forehead, the fine white hair, the loose, wrinkled skin of the hand.

Also working in Leiden at this time was the precociously gifted artist Jan Lievens, who had studied with Lastman a year or two before Rembrandt, and had already established his studio by the time Rembrandt returned from Amsterdam. The two worked closely together, and may even have shared a studio for a time, and it was through Lievens that Rembrandt first came into contact with Constantijn Huygens. Huygens was a courtier and diplomat, served as Secretary to the Stadholder, Prince Frederick Henry of Orange, and was instrumental in getting Rembrandt the commission for the Passion series he worked on between 1632 and 1639. Having commissioned a portrait from Lievens, Huygens visited Leiden in 1629, describing the work of both painters in glowing terms in his autobiography, and it may have been through his recommendation that Rembrandt's study of an old woman found its way into the British Royal Collection.

One of the paintings that Huygens singled out for particular praise was *The Repentant Judas Returning the Thirty Pieces of Silver to the Chief Priests and Elders* (1629), a brilliant exercise in storytelling which both echoes Lastman's concern with the detail of the drama, and prefigures the major narrative work to come. The traitor Judas, despairing and in rags, kneels in supplication before the uncomprehending priests, his fee for betraying Christ thrown down before them. The subject was an unusual one, and x-ray analysis has revealed that Rembrandt made many changes in the composition, both the architectural background and the figure group, in the course of executing the painting.

The greater concern with context and atmosphere hinted at in the depiction of Judas is developed further in one of the last works Rembrandt painted before his departure for Amsterdam, *The Song of Simeon* (1631), in which the aged Simeon recognizes the divinity of Christ when he is presented as a baby in the temple, and lifts up his voice in praise. The work is small-scale, like all Rembrandt's Leiden painting, but behind the brightly lit central group he has created a vast darkened interior which, because the center of action is set further back than in earlier work, seems to draw the viewer into the picture space in a new and powerful way. This grander, more dramatic style forms the basis for the largescale history painting of the 1630s.

Success in Amsterdam: 1630s

In March 1631 Rembrandt bought a plot of land outside the White Gate in Leiden, which does not suggest he intended to leave his home town. It is possible that he went to Amsterdam simply to fulfil a commission, and found himself in such demand that he stayed for the rest of his life. Providently, however, he bought a part share in the business of an Amsterdam art dealer, Hendrick Uylenburgh, and subsequently moved into his house. Uylenburgh seems to have provided materials and possibly studios for young artists in exchange for a profit share of their work which he sold; his relationship with Rembrandt indicates the extent to which painting was a commercial rather than a dilettante activity.

Rembrandt's move to Amsterdam in 1631/32 certainly coincided with his first formal commissioned portrait, and it was as a portraitist that he first found success in what was then the most cosmopolitan city of northern Europe. Although the Stadholder's court was at The Hague, Amsterdam, with its large merchant navy, was the focus of Dutch commercial life and was also fast becoming a center of culture and learning. The population was growing rapidly, and new building was keeping pace with economic expansion. Amsterdam thus offered a much livelier market for a young artist than Leiden and, while Lastman was still at work on religious and mythological subjects, and the portrait painters Nicolaes Eliaszoon and Thomas de Keyser produced sober, unemphatic portraits of the leading citizens, there was no native school of painting as such.

Rembrandt's portrait of *Nicolaes Ruts* (1631) falls at first glance into this conservative tradition. Ruts's prosperity was based on trade with Russia, which included the import of furs, hence perhaps the fur-lined coat and hat. Portraits were charged at a fixed rate, the most expensive being full-length, for which there was little demand in Amsterdam, the three-quarter-length view as here being more popular. Despite the modest style of the portrayal, Rembrandt has achieved a vivid effect, both in Ruts's animated facial expression, and in the sense of movement the portrait conveys. The subject seems to turn back toward the viewer, proffering a letter, a device which Rembrandt uses again in later portraits as

a means of enlivening what might otherwise be a static image.

Another form of portraiture that had become established as an independent category in the course of the sixteenth century was the group portrait, representing a number of men in terms of a common role or function — for example as members of the same profession, or a local militia. With grand history painting out of favor, this was almost the only form of largescale painting available to seventeenth-century Dutch artists, and commissions were much prized. Rembrandt's *The Anatomy Lesson of Dr Nicolaes Tulp* (1632) is one of these, and indicates the prestige that he was already enjoying as a portrait painter. It is also a political statement about the academic status of Amsterdam, where a chair of Anatomy had been established in 1628, with Tulp as the first incumbent, and where a new university opened in the same year that Rembrandt painted Tulp's anatomy class.

The basic problem with this type of representation was to combine a number of portraits of equal individual distinction — each subject paid a proportion of the fee and therefore expected equal prominence — into a coherent whole. Dissections were rare, and therefore treated as festive occasions, with a considerable audience. Earlier paintings on a similar theme had usually consisted of a series of posed figures round a skeleton, skull or head, but Rembrandt transformed the scene into a 'history piece', by showing

FAR LEFT: This drawing, *Self-Portrait with Open Mouth*, c.1628-29, uses the same exaggerated lighting effects as Rembrandt's early painted self-portrait (page 28).

BELOW: *Nicolaes Ruts*, 1631, was one of the first portraits that Rembrandt was commissioned to paint in Amsterdam, and helped to establish his reputation.

the dissection actually in progress. This gives the painting a focus and unity lacking in earlier examples, as the professor begins his dissection with the left arm and his colleagues gather round. In fact a dissection would have begun with the stomach – an essential preliminary as the process could take three days – and so Rembrandt's painting is no more an accurate representation of a real event than those of his predecessors.

The painting was an undoubted success and seems to have led to other commissions; about 50 of his paintings are dated 1632 and 1633, and all but a handful of these are portraits, including a number of double portraits of married couples. Like individual portraiture, this was an innately conservative art form, with the added complication of conveying the relative status of man and woman. In *Jan Rijksen and Griet Jans* (1633), Rembrandt again finds an original solution, by using the delivery of a letter to create an encounter between his two subjects which instantly engages the attention of the viewer. Jan, a shipbuilder, is shown at work in his study and turning to receive a letter which his wife Griet bursts in to deliver. The immediacy of the moment is emphasized by the way Griet keeps hold of the door as she performs her errand.

Rembrandt's sitters were drawn from all ranks of society, but he was particularly at home among the professional classes, notably the Church and medicine, which continued to provide him with commissions throughout his life. Many of the more informal commissions are etched rather than painted. Etching is a form of engraving in which the design is burnt into the plate with acid; it was developed in the early sixteenth century as a shortcut to engraving metal, but soon became an independent art form, and Rembrandt is generally recognized as the greatest etcher of all time. The tradition of the painter-etcher had also been established in the sixteenth century by artists such as Dürer and Mantegna, and Rembrandt explored further the potential of a double career. Initially painting was his principal medium, and etching and drawing took second place, but he soon began to develop both drawing and etching along distinctive paths in order to realize fully the pictorial possibilities of each medium, and certain subjects tend to be explored in one medium rather than another. His attitude to drawing was one of the most original aspects of his practise as an artist. In the Renaissance, drawing had been regarded purely as a preliminary to some more finished piece of work, and Rubens remained firmly in this tradition, but with Rembrandt only a small proportion of his drawings can be seen in this light; most of

them either record his observations or create an imaginary image, and stand as independent works of art.

Some of the most tender and personal drawings and etchings of the 1630s portray Saskia van Uylenburgh, cousin of the art dealer, whom Rembrandt married in 1634. Perhaps the earliest of these is dated in the artist's hand 'the third day of our betrothal, the 8th June 1633,' and shows her half-smiling, wearing a straw hat decorated with flowers and holding a single bloom. The marriage seems to have been a happy one, and Saskia reappears in many drawings of the 1630s. It

ABOVE: Rembrandt's *Portrait of Saskia van Uylenburgh*, 1633, is inscribed 'This is drawn after my wife when she was 21 years old, the 3rd day of our betrothal . . .'

RIGHT: Titian's *Portrait of a Man*, c.1512, influenced Rembrandt's self-portraiture in 1639 and 1640.

14

also represented social advancement for Rembrandt, as Saskia's family were members of the professional class, rather than traders and manufacturers like Rembrandt's relatives. Her father was the mayor of Leewarden in Friesland, two of her brothers were lawyers and the third an army officer.

The couple lived in a succession of houses as Rembrandt's fortunes prospered, finally moving in 1639 into an impressive town house, now the Rembrandthuis, in a fashionable area. In view of the commissions he had received in the previous six or seven years, this did not seem an unreasonable expense, but it in fact marked a turning point in Rembrandt's financial fortunes. The contract specified that he should pay one quarter of the purchase price within a year, with the remainder to be repaid within five years but at an interest rate of five per cent. Rembrandt's name frequently appears as the buyer of works of art at auction sales during these years, and it seems that he and Saskia lived to the limit of their increasingly substantial income. After the death of Saskia's parents, she was accused by one brother of spending her inheritance in a 'flaunting and ostentatious manner', a charge vigorously denied by Rembrandt and Saskia, who maintained that they were 'abundantly blessed with riches.'

The pastoral theme hinted at in the betrothal drawing finds fuller expression in three later paintings, showing her either as an arcadian shepherdess or as the goddess Flora. Of the four children born to Saskia, however, only the last, Titus, survived infancy and outlived his mother, and drawings from the later 1630s show Saskia herself increasingly weary and careworn, and often confined to bed.

The self-portraits that Rembrandt produced during the 1630s also emphasize his worldly success. One in particular, *Self-Portrait at the Age of Thirty-Four* (1640), is interesting for its anachronistic dress; Rembrandt has portrayed himself clothed in sixteenth-century Italian style. Shortly before this was painted, he had attended an auction at which Raphael's *Portrait of Baldassare Castiglione* was sold, and had made a sketch of it. The purchaser was a Spanish merchant, Alfonso Lopez, who was the Amsterdam agent of the French king Louis XIII, and who also owned Titian's *Portrait of a Man*. Both these sixteenth-century portraits seem to have influenced Rembrandt's portrayal of himself; like the Titian, he shows himself facing right and turning to gaze at the viewer, with his right arm resting on a parapet so as to emphasize the rich fabric of his sleeve.

Although renowned in Amsterdam principally as a portrait painter, Rembrandt did not give up history painting, and it is in this rather unfashionable field that his work of the 1630s finds its greatest variety, ranging from the calm and tender mood of *The Holy Family* (c.1634) to the flamboyant drama of *Christ in the Storm on the Sea of Galilee* (1633) or *The Capture and Blinding of Samson* (1636). One particularly notable group of New Testament subjects is worked in grisaille, i.e. entirely in neutral shades rather than full color, and may have been intended as the basis for an ambitious series of etchings. One of the most finely worked of these, *Ecce Homo* (1634), showing Christ being presented by Pilate to the people, is also the only one for which an etching exists as well. The series as a whole shows Rembrandt's narrative skills at their most powerful. In *Saint John the Baptist Preaching* (1634), the central figure of St John dominates a richly diverse and carefully marshaled crowd, which includes Indians and Japanese, Pharisees and Sadducees, peasants and merchants, children and dogs, their attitudes ranging from enthralment to sleep.

It was the Old Testament, however, that provoked the most vivid and violent

paintings of the 1630s. The grander and more dramatic style of the early Amsterdam years reflects a move away from the narrative detail of Lastman and shows Rembrandt freshly inspired by the action and violence of some of Caravaggio's and Rubens's paintings. Perhaps the most extreme of these is *The Capture and Blinding of Samson* (1636), which shows in grotesque and yet horribly convincing detail the pain of Samson's blinding by the Philistines, after he has told the treacherous Delilah the secret of his strength. Lit low and from the left, the huge canvas is a confusion of violent contrasts: light and shadow, struggle and vicious restraint, brilliant color and deepest blackness, unbearable pain and gloating triumph. *Belshazzar's Feast* (c.1636–38), painted a year or so later, follows similar principles, in its use of violent movement, selective lighting and intense emotion to capture a moment of exaggerated drama. Reflecting Lastman's attention to accurate detail, Rembrandt follows the text of the *Book of Daniel* closely in portraying the richness of the scene, the gold and silver looted from the temple of Jerusalem, and the horror of the Babylonian king

Belshazzar and his guests as the miraculous hand inscribes his doom on the palace wall. It was an unusual subject, and Rembrandt took full advantage of the opportunity it afforded for rhetoric.

Other history paintings of the 1630s show an altogether gentler side of the artist's nature. As well as religious themes, he also etched and painted mythological subjects, and seems to have taken a particular interest in the hunter goddess Diana. An etching showing *Diana at the Bath* (c.1631), for which the preparatory drawing also exists, is Rembrandt's earliest fully worked nude study, a new development that culminates in the glorious *Bathsheba* of 1654. Another nude depiction from a little later in the 1630s has been given the title *Danaë*, and certainly the inventory of Rembrandt's possessions made in 1656 includes a painting of that name. Danaë was one of Jupiter's many lovers; he gained access to the prison in which her jealous father had locked her by transforming himself into a shower of gold. More disturbing, and perhaps closer in mood to the savage Old Testament works, is a more ambitious mythological subject, *The Rape of Ganymede* (1635). A beautiful youth whom the wilful Jupiter, this time in the form of an eagle, carried off to become his cup-bearer, Ganymede in Rembrandt's depiction is a plump and furiously crying child, who urinates as he is unceremoniously torn by the eagle from his familiar environment.

The most important commission that Rembrandt received in the 1630s, one of his very rare commissions for a history, and one that took him most of the decade to complete, almost certainly came about through the benign influence of Constantijn Huygens. In 1632 Rembrandt was employed to paint the portrait of the Stadholder's wife, Amalia van Solms, as a pendant to a portrait of the prince himself painted by the fashionable international artist Gerrit van Honthorst. A year later Rembrandt received a much more substantial commission, a cycle of five scenes from the life and passion of Christ. Of these the first two were painted in 1633, and three more were finished between 1635 and 1639.

The first of the series, *The Descent from the Cross* (1633), may have been an independent work and the stimulus for the commission. Modeled on one panel of the triptych which Rubens had painted for Antwerp Cathedral about 20 years earlier, it nonetheless strikes a quite different note. In both works the body of Christ is lowered from the cross by means of a cloth, with a grieving crowd looking on, but in Rubens's depiction, the helpers and the mourning women frame the body and draw the eye, with their richly colored garments and eloquent gestures, while Rembrandt, with a more muted use of color and emptier canvas, uses the shroud as a foil against which the realistically slumped body of Christ becomes the focus of the painting. The second painting in the Passion series, *The Raising of the Cross* (1633), was finished and delivered at much the same time.

The only letters that survive in Rembrandt's hand relate to this series. Unfortunately these are far from informative about the character of the artist, being businesslike and deferential in tone. In one of them, however, in which Rembrandt apologizes for the late delivery of the first two paintings, he makes his only reference to his credo as a painter, explaining that the work took so long because he 'concentrated on expressing the most natural movement.' A pause of three years then ensued, and the correspondence attests to the displeasure this caused Huygens. In 1636 Rembrandt wrote that he was 'very diligently engaged in completing as quickly as possible the three Passion pictures which His Excellency himself commissioned me to do . . .' The first of these, *The Ascension of Christ*, seems to have been delivered shortly thereafter. Finally, on 12 January 1639, Rembrandt writes that 'because of the great zeal and devotion which I exercised in executing well the two pictures which His Highness commissioned me to make . . . these same two pictures have now been finished through serious application.' These were *The Entombment of Christ* and *The Resurrection of Christ* (both 1635–39). While the Resurrection is shown as an almost chaotic incident, with the soldiers left to guard the body of Christ fleeing pellmell from the triumphant angel, the Entombment has a more serene and contemplative mood which presages the new direction Rembrandt was to take in the 1640s.

LEFT: This etching of *Diana at the Bath*, c.1631, is Rembrandt's earliest fully worked nude study.

RIGHT: The decline in Saskia's health is touchingly charted in the drawings of the 1630s and early 1640s. *Saskia Sitting by a Window* dates from 1638, only five years after the carefree betrothal portrait. Saskia died in 1642, shortly after giving birth to the couple's fourth, and only surviving, child.

For each of the first two pictures Rembrandt had been paid 600 guilders, but in 1639 he wrote hopefully to Huygens that the last two 'will be considered of such quality that His Highness will now even pay me not less than a thousand guilders each.' Neither response nor any payment was forthcoming, however, and the first payment on what is now the Rembrandthuis was coming due, so Rembrandt wrote again, asking that 'Whatever His Highness grants me for the two pieces, I may receive this money as soon as possible, which would at the moment be particularly convenient to me.' He was finally paid, at the original price of 600 guilders per painting, and this is the last known contact between him and Huygens. Whether displeased at his protégé's change of style, or irritated by his importuning for payment, Huygens totally ignored Rembrandt for the remaining 30 years of his life, playing no part in the commission from the Stadholder for two further paintings in the 1640s.

A Change of Direction: 1640s and 1650s

The quieter, more restrained style of Rembrandt's maturity is forecast in his Titian-inspired *Self-portrait at the Age of Thirty-Four* (1640), already discussed. Some commentators have suggested that in this painting Rembrandt was not only consciously comparing his own achievement with that of a famous painter of the past, but also making a clear statement about the dignity and standing of the artist, still sometimes regarded more as craftsman than as an original creator in his own right. The solemn elegance with which he depicts himself implies equality with any viewer, and this more personal, self-analytical style was to prove the touchstone of his mature work. The development was a gradual one, but in the course of the 1640s Rembrandt slowly turned away from much that his painting had stood for in the previous decade, abandoning baroque display in favor of classical simplicity, and attempting to convey a sense of man's spiritual rather than his active life. This effectively removed him from the sphere of fashionable taste, and commissions became rarer as his work became increasingly individual and contemplative.

In part this development may have been motivated by personal experience. As well as financial troubles, Rembrandt had to bear the early deaths of his first three children, and the slow decline of Saskia, movingly documented in a series of drawings and etchings. She finally died in 1642, only nine months after the birth of their only surviving child, Titus. One manifestation of this change of mood and new solitude is Rembrandt's novel exploration of landscape as a subject in its own right. Between about 1640 and

1655, he produced a large number of etchings and drawings, and the occasional painting, which depict in carefully observed detail not just an impersonalized landscape, but a specific and recognizable locality. He investigated and analyzed the city of Amsterdam and its environs with extraordinary intensity, and the gradual simplification of his style, in order to express a newly introspective mood, can be traced in the development of his landscape studies, from fully realized and worked up prints and drawings at the outset, to late scenes vividly delineated with no more than a few strokes of the brush.

This growing simplicity and tranquillity is also observable in Rembrandt's choice of subject-matter in the 1640s. While the concern with history painting, and above all with biblical scenes, continues, the themes chosen are reflective moments, indicative of character and quiet emotion, rather than the grand demonstrations of earlier works. In the life of Christ, the moments shown relate to Christ's infancy rather than his Passion, and develop the theme of idealized domesticity that had earlier found expression in secular scenes, and above all in depictions of Saskia. Thus *The Holy Family with Painted Frame and Curtain* (1646) shows the Virgin leaning lovingly over an animated baby, who is perhaps resisting the bedtime implied by the crib at his mother's right. A small fire provides the only light, playing on the group formed by Virgin and Child and warming both the Virgin's bare feet and a disreputable-looking cat, while the background is shrouded in an almost impenetrable gloom in which Joseph can just be discerned at right, cutting wood.

Drawings and etchings from this period echo this peaceable domestic atmosphere, and it is significant that when Prince Frederick Henry commissioned two more scenes from the life of Christ, the subjects Rembrandt chose were a *Nativity* and a *Circumcision*. He finally achieved the price he wanted, for the Stadholder's account books record a

payment of 2400 guilders for these in 1646. The *Circumcision* is lost, but the *Nativity*, more accurately *The Adoration of the Shepherds*, survives, painted on canvas instead of panel. Although the same size as the five Passion scenes, it is both quieter and more intimate in mood. It is also worked up in a looser manner, in which the texture of the paint seems to have a life of its own, almost unrelated to the forms it describes and quite different from the precision with which details were defined in the earlier paintings.

The quest for a new style is vividly demonstrated in an etching known as the 'Hundred Guilder Print', which does not show a single event, but rather a series of episodes from Christ's ministry as described in the Gospel of Saint Matthew, and which Rembrandt seems to have worked on over a lengthy period in the 1640s. The many alterations to both style and subject would have required long and laborious work on a single plate, and it is characteristic of Rembrandt's doggedness that he did not abandon it. The initial conception was grandiose, with a large cast skilfully arranged around the figure of Christ, in a fashion reminiscent of *Saint John the Baptist Preaching* (c.1634), but as the work progressed, individual figures and interactions were given more weight. Thus in the right foreground the sick come to be healed; to the left are the Pharisees with whom Jesus debated the nature of marriage; in front of them a mother presents her infant for Christ's blessing. Finally, to Christ's left kneels the rich youth who sought eternal life, to be told that it was easier for a camel to pass through the eye of a needle than for a rich man to enter the Kingdom of God — the camel seen through the archway at far right emphasizes the point. As Rembrandt made his subject more diverse and complex, he also varied the chiaroscuro to heighten individual figures or incidents and yet create an overall pattern which radiates from the central figure of Christ.

Following this development, Rembrandt's etchings of the 1650s rework New Testament subjects in a manner that is nothing less than revolutionary. In perhaps the most powerful of all of these, *The Three Crosses* (1653, reworked in three more different states) he returns to the climax of the Passion of Christ in a monumental and terrifying fashion. The arrangement of the main figures, with Jesus crucified centrally and the thieves to left and right, follows traditional iconography, but the attendant figures — Romans and Jewish elders, the centurion, the Magdalen clasping the base of the cross, the swooning Virgin, St John behind her looking up at Christ, and a number of other unidentified figures in various states of shock and fear — again fall naturally into a series of discrete groups. Most of them are only summarily sketched, and the overwhelming, unifying element in the whole scene is the cone of light, which not only pulls the composition into a coherent whole, but also itself acts as a part of the narrative, focusing on the blessed and leaving the unbelievers in semi-darkness.

As a biblical painter, Rembrandt created a new kind of art by his ability to grasp the essence of a human situation and convey it with intense yet undramatized feeling. Whereas in the 1630s he had focused on the heroes of the Old Testament, the moments of drama and deliverance, in his later work it is the relationship between the figures he portrays which interests him; there is little or no action or external excitement. One of the Old Testament themes which preoccupied him in later years, mainly in the form of drawings and prints, was that of David; the oil of *Bathsheba with King David's Letter* (1654) is a rare incursion into paint. Echoing earlier works in its use of a letter to give point to the image, it is nonetheless quite different in mood, with the pensive Bathsheba contemplating the contents of the letter she holds, oblivious to the elderly attendant who

dries her feet. Most previous depictions of Bathsheba had shown David spying on her as she bathed, but Rembrandt focuses on her moment of doubt and indecision as she receives the king's invitation. Her figure dominates the composition, and the rich warm colors reflect Rembrandt's interest in sixteenth-century Venetian art, which is traceable in other works of the 1650s.

Perhaps the most moving and delicate of all these late Bible paintings is *Jacob Blessing the Sons of Joseph* (1656), in which the aged patriarch chooses to bless the younger son first, recognizing his higher destiny. Again Rembrandt breaks with the traditional mode of representing this theme, in which Joseph tries to correct his father. Here any altercation is over; Joseph watches approvingly, as does the boys' mother Asenath, not even mentioned in the Bible account. Rembrandt focuses on the tender relationship between the figures, stressing its significance to each participant. The intensely spiritual atmosphere is enhanced by a glow of light that seems to emanate from the figures themselves. The composition is concentrated in the foreground and the spatial setting is almost non-existent; nothing distracts the eye from the moment of benediction so touchingly conveyed. The distance between this tranquil, personal work and, for example, the drama and excitement of *Belshazzar's Feast*, marks the extent of Rembrandt's unique and, in the context of mid-seventeenth-century Dutch art, lonely development.

Although he never again achieved the contemporary acclaim of the 1630s, however, some commissions did continue to come Rembrandt's way. One of the most important of these, and perhaps Rembrandt's best known work, is the erroneously titled *The Night Watch* (1642), more accurately *The Company of Frans Banning Cocq Preparing to March Out*. The subject, a group portrait of the militia company of *arquebusiers* or

musketeers, who had their headquarters a few doors from Rembrandt's and Saskia's house, is a conventional one, but Rembrandt's approach to it is not. Instead of a series of individual posed portraits, he has approached the composition with the instinct of a history painter, allowing the group to dominate and showing it not artificially posed but responding to a call to arms. The captain makes a gesture of command as he and his lieutenant set off, provoking a controled chaos of movement behind them as the rest of the company prepare to follow and an audience of children and dogs looks on.

Group portraiture continued to inspire some of Rembrandt's most substantial and impressive works until the very end of his life. In 1656 he again painted the Amsterdam Group of Surgeons, under their leader Dr Joan Deyman, successor to Nicholaes Tulp. This survives only in a fragmentary state, enough to demonstrate that it was no less revolutionary in conception than *The Night Watch*. The corpse is shown dramatically foreshortened, with its feet seeming to pro-

trude out of the picture space, and this time the stomach cavity is empty; Rembrandt was better informed about the process of dissection by now. Rembrandt's final excursion into group portraiture, *The Sampling Officials of the Drapers' Guild (The Syndics)* of 1662, shows the five men responsible for inspecting cloth samples grouped round a sample book on a table, and looking toward the viewer as though just interrupted in their discussion. X-ray analysis has revealed that Rembrandt made considerable alterations to the position of some of the figures before he was satisfied that he had made a unified composition. Their varied poses prevent the work from seeming regimented, and the rich red of the carpet draped over the table provides an effective color contrast to the somber black and white of the men's dress.

Occasional commissions for single portraits also came Rembrandt's way in the 1640s and 1650s. The *Portrait of Agatha Bas* (1641) is one of his most convincing and tender characterizations, while his painting of the wealthy cloth merchant

Jan Six (1654) has been hailed as the most beautiful ever painted, combining painterly technique with psychological insight. Like so many of Rembrandt's portraits, an effect of immediacy is achieved by showing the subject in the act of drawing on a glove, and this is reinforced by the swift confident brushstrokes, which capture the fall of light, the rich texture of the clothes, and the movement of the hands. The composition is daring, with the brilliantly-cloaked figure of Six shown off-center, head tilted reflectively forward as he gazes assessingly directly at the viewer. Further evidence that, despite his relative lack of local success, Rembrandt's reputation as a painter was widespread at this time comes from the group of works he produced for the Sicilian nobleman Don Antonio Ruffo, who in 1652 commissioned a portrait of a philosopher, now known as *Aristotle Contemplating the Bust of Homer*.

After Saskia's death, Rembrandt employed a nurse, Geertje Dircx, to look after the young Titus, and it seems that

19

The Last Years: 1660s

In his maturity, Rembrandt's mastery of the techniques of painting, drawing and etching not only gave him complete freedom of expression, whatever his subject, but also enabled him to vary both subject and style in a way that makes his late work almost impossible to classify. As his search for the heart of a particular subject became both more perceptive and more personal, so each work posed its own unique problems and required its own specific solutions. What is clear is that he withdrew more and more into his own imagination; the last decade saw no landscapes, few figure studies and fewer genre scenes. What does unite these late paintings is an extraordinarily free technique, in which at times the paint is built up with a palette knife into an almost sculptural density, while at times it is just skimmed across the canvas with the lightest of touches. On examination, what appears to be a hand or a sleeve disintegrates, and yet the overall pictorial logic remains.

This highly individual approach seems to have been increasingly out of step with contemporary trends and, apart from the group portrait *The Sampling Officials of the Drapers' Guild* (1662) and a few single portraits, such as that of *Jacob Trip* (1661) and the grand equestrian portrait of *Frederick Rihel* (1663), his only substantial commission was for a history painting for the new City Hall in Amsterdam. Rembrandt's former pupil Govaert Flinck had been the first choice for this, and when he died the job was divided between Rembrandt, Lievens and Jacob Jordaens. The city fathers wanted a series of canvases on a single theme celebrating Dutch independence, to be set into lunettes around the large gallery surrounding the main hall. The subject chosen was the revolt of the Batavians, regarded by the Dutch as their forerunners, against the Romans, under their leader Claudius Civilis. Rembrandt was given the first scene, showing the banquet at which Civilis and his fellow-conspirators swear to oust the Romans. In its original form, *The Conspiracy of Claudius Civilis* was larger than *The Night Watch* and the most monumental work of Rembrandt's entire oeuvre; it should have been a fitting conclusion to a career that coincided with the triumphant emergence of the Dutch Republic. The painting only survives in a fragmentary state, however, because within a year of its installation in the City Hall it had been removed, cut down (presumably by the artist himself to make it more saleable) and replaced with the work of a much inferior painter, Jurriaen Ovens. Flinck's preparatory drawing had shown the conspirators clasping hands in the Roman manner, whereas Rembrandt shows the

she became his lover, and probably also his model, although no likeness has firmly been identified. In 1649, however, the relationship ended acrimoniously and she was dismissed. In retaliation, she brought a breach of promise suit against Rembrandt in the Court of Matrimonial Causes, citing as a pledge the jewelry he had rashly given her, and was awarded an annuity of 200 guilders for life. Rembrandt's representative before the court was Hendrickje Stoffels, and she seems to have taken Geertje's place in Rembrandt's household – and his affections. Their daughter Cornelia was born in 1654, in the same year that Hendrickje was castigated by the Council of the Reformed Church for her unorthodox relationship with the artist. Although no documented likeness of Hendrickje exists, an affectionately depicted model reappears regularly during the 1650s who has been tentatively identified as her. One of these, the small and rapidly executed *Woman Bathing* (1654), is among Rembrandt's most tender and sensitive depictions.

Despite this evidence of domestic harmony, the 1650s heralded growing financial difficulties for Rembrandt. The year 1653 marked the worst of an economic downturn in Dutch affairs due to reversals in the First Anglo-Dutch War, which led to near financial collapse in Amsterdam. Rembrandt still owed just over half the price of his house, and had paid no interest on the outstanding amount for five years. Pressed to settle the debt, he took out several loans to do so, but in May 1656 was clearly again in trouble. In an effort to save the house, he appeared before the Court of Orphans and transferred the title into Titus's name, but by July his position was so precarious that he was forced to apply for a form of voluntary bankruptcy. This avoided the possibility of debtor's prison and enabled him to keep enough of his earnings to support his family, but all his property was auctioned. The surviving inventory provides a fascinating record both of Rembrandt's collection of paintings, which was substantial and wide-ranging, and of the furnishings and minutiae of his domestic life. The house itself was sold in 1658, but it was only in 1661 that Rembrandt satisfied the court that he had met all his obligations and was free of all restriction.

As with the painful years of the early 1640s, however, this traumatic chain of events did not have a deleterious effect on his skill as a painter; in fact the reverse seems to have been the case, and the paintings of the last decade of his life, right up until his death in the fall of 1669, show a growing profundity and grandeur.

oath being made as the Roman historian Tacitus described, according to *barbaro ritu*, with sword tips joined. Rather than a heroic band of deliverers, he shows the Batavians as an all-too-convincing bunch of ruffians and accurately represents Civilis with only one eye. The city fathers may have felt that a greater degree of classical decorum, as against historical accuracy, was more consonant with the sober elegance of their new City Hall.

If the public proved unappreciative, Rembrandt's private world in these last years seems to have been a stable and loving one. Hendrickje remained his devoted companion until her death in 1663; when the Guild of St Luke, the painters' trade union, introduced a regulation that any member who had sold up could not continue to trade in Amsterdam, she and Titus formed a company, with Rembrandt as its employee, so that they could continue to market his work. In 1668 Titus married Magdalena van Loo, an old family friend whose father had testified on Rembrandt's behalf at the time of his insolvency, and it has been suggested that the touchingly devoted couple portrayed in the curiously titled painting *The Jewish Bride* (*c*.1665–68) may reflect their happiness. The same model who posed for the bride seems to reappear in a probably slightly later painting, *A Family Group* (*c*.1668).

Within seven months of his marriage Titus was dead, and six months later Magdalena gave birth to a daughter, Titia. It is perhaps not surprising that in his very last works Rembrandt reverts to the self-scrutiny that had always run like a thread through his painting. His self-portraits reach a new peak in the last 20 years of his life and, though neglected by his immediate successors, are now viewed as a major element in his oeuvre. As was the general practise in the seventeenth century, some, in more severely self-analytical mode, show him without attributes, while others, the minority, focus on his role as artist. The *Self-Portrait* of 1655, for example, dates from one of the most difficult periods of his life financially, and this is perhaps reflected in the unforgiving analysis of this closely observed face. In 1658, on the other hand, he portrays himself in the kind of 'costume-piece' that had interested him in the 1630s, magisterially robed and holding a staff of office; in 1660 he shows himself, more conventionally, as an artist, palette and brushes in hand; in 1661 he appears as the apostle St Paul; and in 1668, the year both of Titus's marriage and his death, one of the most extraordinary and personal of these self-portraits shows him laughing.

Rembrandt continued to paint until immediately before his own death, which followed that of his son by little more than a year, although much that he worked on remained unfinished. The two self-portraits that survive from this last year abandon the various roles he had played and show him simply as a weary but still determined and independent old man. All the observation and humanity that he had brought 30 years earlier to the depiction of old age is suffused with a personal dignity and a serene acceptance that make these final self-portraits among the most poignant and immediate works of his entire career.

After Titus's marriage, Rembrandt continued to live in the small house to which he, Hendrickje and Titus had moved in 1658, with Cornelia, his daughter by Hendrickje. The inventory drawn up the day after his death, on 4 October 1669, lists 50 items, mainly of furniture and domestic equipment, as against the 363 items including works of art in the sale list of 1656. A mere six weeks after Rembrandt, Magdalena too died, leaving the two orphans, fifteen-year-old daughter Cornelia and infant grand-daughter Titia, as the sole survivors. Titia later married her guardian's son and died without issue in 1725; Cornelia married the year after her father's death, and called her two children Rembrandt and Hendrickje.

Although he died in relative obscurity, Rembrandt continued to have admirers after his death, and his work often fetched high prices in the eighteenth century. His mastery of light and shade was recognized, but most critics considered him a flawed and undisciplined genius. It was the age of Romanticism that first hailed the intensely personal and emotional nature of his art. In 1851 the great French Romantic painter Eugène Delacroix suggested that Rembrandt would one day be rated higher than Raphael; 'a piece of blasphemy that will make every good academician's hair stand on end.' The prophesy came true within 50 years.

FAR LEFT: This composite diagram shows Rembrandt's *The Conspiracy of Claudius Civilis*, 1661, superimposed on his sketch of the original design.

BELOW: *Self-Portrait, Drawing at a Window*, etching, 1648.

Above:
THE STONING OF SAINT STEPHEN, 1625
Oil on wood,
35 × 48¼ inches (89.5 × 123.6 cm)
Musée des Beaux-Arts, Lyon

Right:
TOBIT AND ANNA WITH THE KID, 1626
Oil on wood,
15⅝ × 11⅝ inches (40.1 × 29.9 cm)
Rijksmuseum, Amsterdam

THE RICH MAN FROM THE PARABLE, 1627
Oil on wood,
12½ × 16⅝ inches (31.9 × 42.5 cm)
Gemäldegalerie, Berlin

CHRIST AT EMMAUS, *c.*1628
Oil on paper stuck to wood,
14⅝ × 16½ inches (37.4 × 42.3 cm)
Musée Jacquemart-André, Paris

26

SELF-PORTRAIT, *c.*1628
Oil on wood,
8¾ × 7¼ inches (22.5 × 18.6 cm)
Rijksmuseum, Amsterdam

SELF-PORTRAIT, *c.*1629
Oil on wood,
14¾ × 11¼ inches (37.9 × 28.9 cm)
The Mauritshuis, The Hague

THE ARTIST IN HIS STUDIO, *c.*1629
Oil on wood,
9¾ × 12½ inches (25.1 × 31.9 cm)
Museum of Fine Arts, Boston

THE REPENTANT JUDAS RETURNING THE THIRTY
PIECES OF SILVER TO THE CHIEF PRIESTS AND
ELDERS, 1629
Oil on wood,
30⅝ × 40 inches (79 × 102.3 cm)
Private collection, England

Left:
AN OLD WOMAN: 'THE ARTIST'S MOTHER,'
*c.*1629
Oil on wood,
23⅝ × 18½ inches (61 × 47.4 cm)
Royal Collection, Windsor Castle

Above:
JEREMIAH LAMENTING THE DESTRUCTION OF
JERUSALEM, 1630
Oil on wood,
22¾ × 18¼ inches (58.3 × 46.6 cm)
Rijksmuseum, Amsterdam

THE PROPHETESS ANNA, 1631
Oil on wood,
23⅜ × 18⅝ inches (59.8 × 47.7 cm)
Rijksmuseum, Amsterdam

THE SONG OF SIMEON, 1631
Oil on wood,
23¾ × 18⅝ inches (60.9 × 47.8 cm)
The Mauritshuis, The Hague

Left:
A MAN IN A GORGET AND PLUMED CAP, *c.*1631
(Rembrandt's circle)
Oil on wood,
21⅝ × 20 inches (56 × 51 cm)
J Paul Getty Museum, Malibu

Above:
MAN IN ORIENTAL COSTUME
('THE NOBLE SLAV'), 1632
Oil on canvas,
59⅝ × 43⅜ inches (152.7 × 111.1 cm)
Metropolitan Museum of Art, New York

39

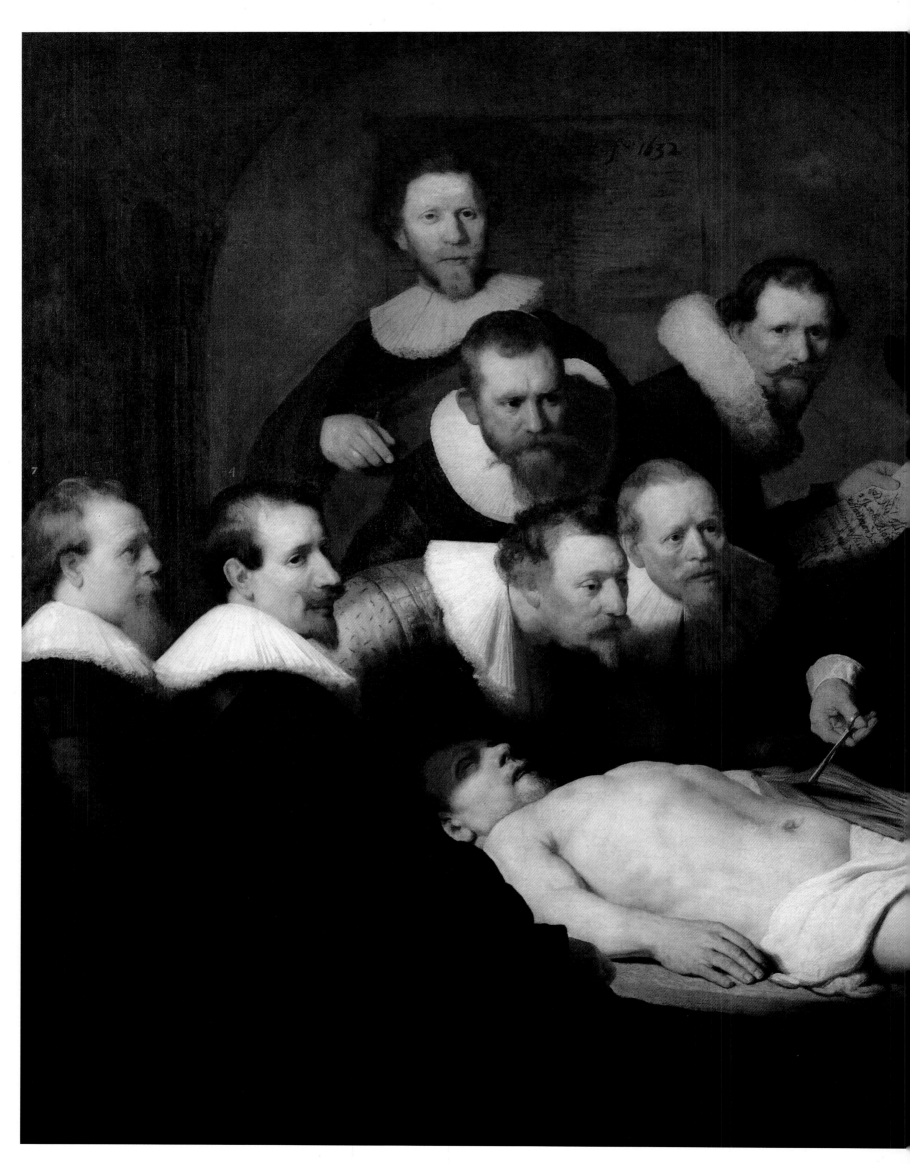

THE ANATOMY LESSON OF DR NICOLAES TULP,
1632
Oil on canvas,
66¼ × 84½ inches (169.5 × 216.5 cm)
The Mauritshuis, The Hague

41

JAN RIJKSEN AND GRIET JANS, 1633
Oil on canvas,
44⅝ × 66 inches (114.3 × 168.9 cm)
Royal Collection, Buckingham Palace

Above: THE RAISING OF THE CROSS, *c.*1633
Oil on canvas,
37½ × 28¼ inches (96.2 × 72.2 cm)
Alte Pinakothek, Munich

Right: THE DESCENT FROM THE CROSS, *c.*1633
Oil on wood,
34⅞ × 25½ inches (89.4 × 65.2 cm)
Alte Pinakothek, Munich

CHRIST IN THE STORM ON THE SEA OF GALILEE, 1633
Oil on canvas,
62½ × 49⅝ inches (160 × 127 cm)
Isabella Stewart Gardner Museum, Boston

FREDERICK RIHEL ON HORSEBACK, *c.*1663
Oil on canvas,
115 × 94⅛ inches (294.5 × 241 cm)
The National Gallery, London

THE LAMENTATION AT THE FOOT OF THE CROSS, *c*.1634-35
Pen and ink and wash with chalk, reworked in oil,
8½ × 9 inches (21.6 × 25.4 cm)
British Museum, London

PORTRAIT OF AN EIGHTY-THREE-YEAR-OLD WOMAN, 1634
Oil on wood,
27¾ × 21⅝ inches (71.1 × 55.9 cm)
The National Gallery, London

Left:
THE HOLY FAMILY, *c.*1634
Oil on canvas,
71⅝ × 48 inches (183.5 × 123 cm)
Alte Pinakothek, Munich

Above:
THE RISEN CHRIST APPEARING TO MARY
MAGDALEN, 1638
Oil on wood,
23⅝ × 19⅜ inches (61 × 49.5 cm)
Royal Collection, Buckingham Palace

SAINT JOHN THE BAPTIST PREACHING, *c.*1634
Oil on canvas laid on panel,
24¼ × 31¼ inches (62 × 80 cm)
Staatliche Museen Preussischer Kulturbesitz,
Gemäldegalerie, Berlin

ECCE HOMO, 1634
Oil on paper stuck on canvas,
21¼ × 17⅜ inches (54.4 × 44.5 cm)
The National Gallery, London

FLORA, 1635
Oil on canvas,
48¼ × 38 inches (123.5 × 97.5 cm)
The National Gallery, London

DANAË, 1636
Oil on canvas,
64½ × 79¼ inches (185 × 203 cm)
The Hermitage, St Petersburg

Above:
THE LAMENTATION OVER THE DEAD CHRIST,
c.1635
Oil on paper and canvas mounted on oak,
12½ × 10½ inches (31.9 × 26.7 cm)
The National Gallery, London

Right:
THE RAPE OF GANYMEDE, 1635
Oil on canvas,
66¾ × 50¾ inches (171 × 130 cm)
Gemäldegalerie, Dresden

THE CAPTURE AND BLINDING OF SAMSON, 1636
Oil on canvas,
80 × 106¼ inches (205 × 272 cm)
Städelsches Kunstinstitut, Frankfurt

BELSHAZZAR'S FEAST, *c.*1636-38
Oil on canvas,
65½ × 81¾ inches (167.6 × 209.2 cm)
The National Gallery, London

Above:
PHILIPS LUCASZ., 1635
Oil on wood,
31 × 23 inches (79.5 × 58.9 cm)
The National Gallery, London

Right:
PORTRAIT OF A MAN, STANDING, 1639
Oil on canvas,
78¼ × 48½ inches (200 × 124.2 cm)
Gemäldegalerie, Kassel

Left:
THE ANGEL LEAVING TOBIAS AND HIS FAMILY, 1637
Oil on panel,
26½ × 20¼ inches (68 × 52 cm)
Musée du Louvre, Paris

Above:
THE ENTOMBMENT OF CHRIST, *c.* 1639
Oil on wood,
12½ × 15¾ inches (32.2 × 40.5 cm)
Hunterian Museum and Art Gallery, Glasgow

LANDSCAPE WITH A STONE BRIDGE, *c.*1638
Oil on wood,
11½ × 16⅝ inches (29.5 × 42.5 cm)
Rijksmuseum, Amsterdam

STILL LIFE WITH TWO DEAD PEACOCKS AND A GIRL, *c.* 1639
Oil on canvas,
56⅝ × 52⅞ inches (145 × 135.5 cm)
Rijksmuseum, Amsterdam

SELF-PORTRAIT AT THE AGE OF THIRTY-FOUR, 1640
Oil on canvas,
39⅞ × 31¼ inches (102 × 80 cm)
The National Gallery, London

PORTRAIT OF AGATHA BAS, 1641
Oil on canvas,
41 × 32¾ inches (105.2 × 83.9 cm)
Royal Collection, Buckingham Palace

THE COMPANY OF FRANS BANNING COCQ
PREPARING TO MARCH OUT,
KNOWN AS 'THE NIGHT WATCH,' 1642
Oil on canvas,
141¾ × 170¾ inches (363 × 437 cm)
*On loan from the City of Amsterdam to the
Rijksmuseum, Amsterdam*

GIRL LEANING ON A WINDOWSILL, 1645
Oil on canvas,
31⅞ × 25¾ inches (81.6 × 66 cm)
Dulwich Picture Gallery, London

WINTER LANDSCAPE, 1646
Oil on wood,
6⅝ × 9 inches (17 × 23 cm)
Gemäldegalerie, Kassel

THE HOLY FAMILY WITH A PAINTED FRAME
AND CURTAIN, 1646
Oil on wood,
18⅛ × 26⅞ inches (46.5 × 68.8 cm)
Gemäldegalerie, Kassel

THE ADORATION OF THE SHEPHERDS, 1646
Oil on canvas,
25½ × 21½ inches (65.5 × 55 cm)
The National Gallery, London

THE WOMAN TAKEN IN ADULTERY, *c.*1646
Oil on wood,
32½ × 25⅛ inches (83.3 × 64.4 cm)
The National Gallery, London

Susanna and The Elders, 1647
Oil on wood, 29⅝ × 35½ inches (76 × 91 cm)
Staatliche Museen Preussischer Kulturbesitz,
Gemäldegalerie, Berlin

ARISTOTLE CONTEMPLATING THE BUST OF HOMER, 1653
Oil on canvas,
55⅞ × 53¼ inches (143 × 136 cm)
The Metropolitan Museum of Art, New York

Left:
A WOMAN BATHING, 1654
Oil on wood,
24⅛ × 18⅜ inches (61.8 × 47 cm)
The National Gallery, London

Above:
FLORA, *c.*1654
Oil on canvas,
39 × 35⅞ inches (100 × 91.8 cm)
The Metropolitan Museum of Art, New York

BATHSHEBA WITH KING DAVID'S LETTER, 1654
Oil on canvas,
55½ × 55½ inches (142 × 142 cm)
Musée du Louvre, Paris

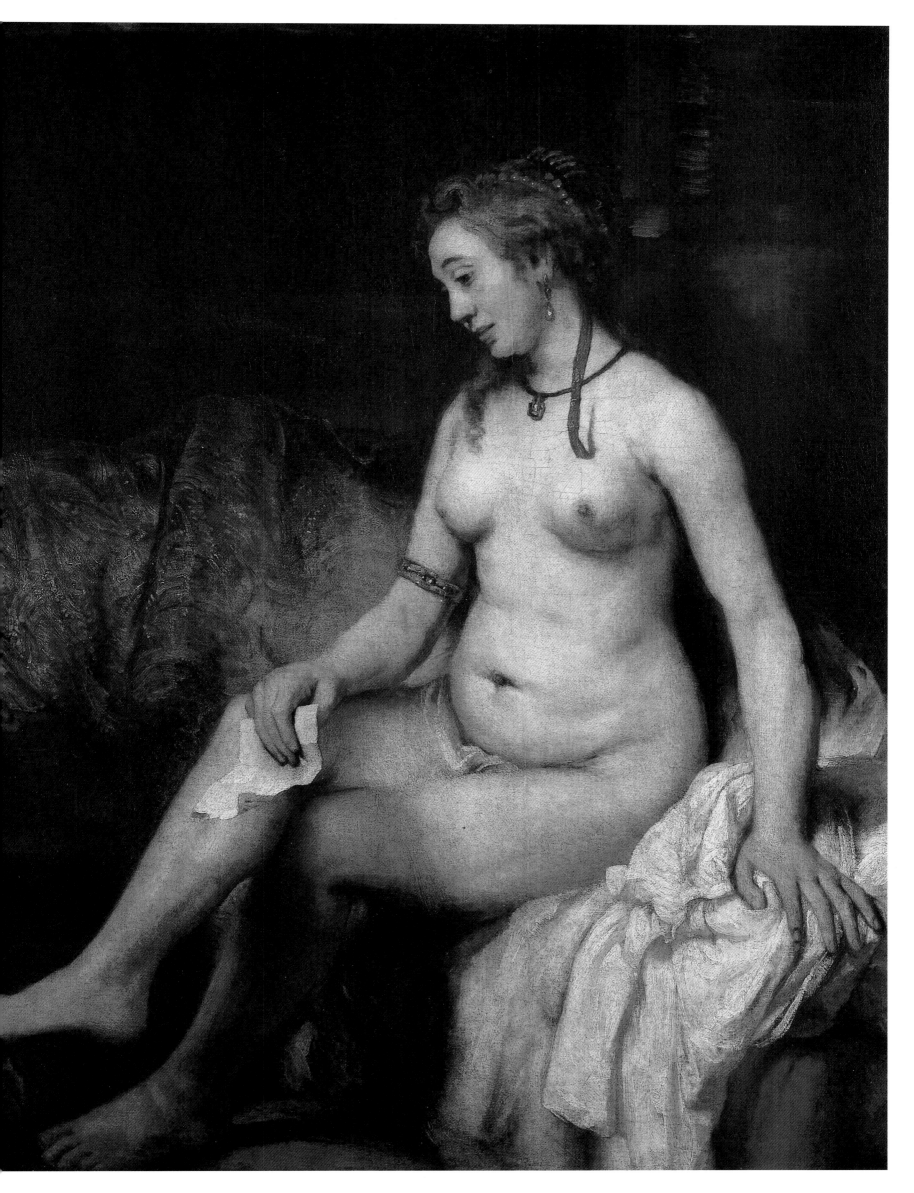

Above:
JAN SIX, 1654
Oil on canvas,
43¾ × 39⅞ inches (112 × 102 cm)
Six Collection, Amsterdam

An Old Woman Reading, 1655
Oil on canvas,
31¼ × 25¾ inches (80 × 66 cm)
Collection of the Duke of Buccleuch,
Drumlanrig Castle, Scotland

TITUS AT HIS DESK, 1655
Oil on canvas,
30 × 24½ inches (77 × 63 cm)
Museum Boymans-van Beuningen, Rotterdam

Above:
SELF-PORTRAIT, *c.*1655
Oil on wood,
19¼ × 16 inches (49.2 × 41 cm)
Kunsthistorisches Museum, Vienna

Right:
WOMAN AT AN OPEN DOOR
(HENDRICKJE STOFFELS?), *c.*1656
Oil on canvas,
34½ × 26⅛ inches (88.5 × 67 cm)
Staatliche Museen Preussischer Kulturbesitz,
Gemäldegalerie, Berlin

THE ANATOMY LECTURE OF DR JOAN DEYMAN,
1656
Oil on canvas,
39 × 52⅜ inches (100 × 134 cm)
On loan from the City of Amsterdam to the
Rijksmuseum, Amsterdam

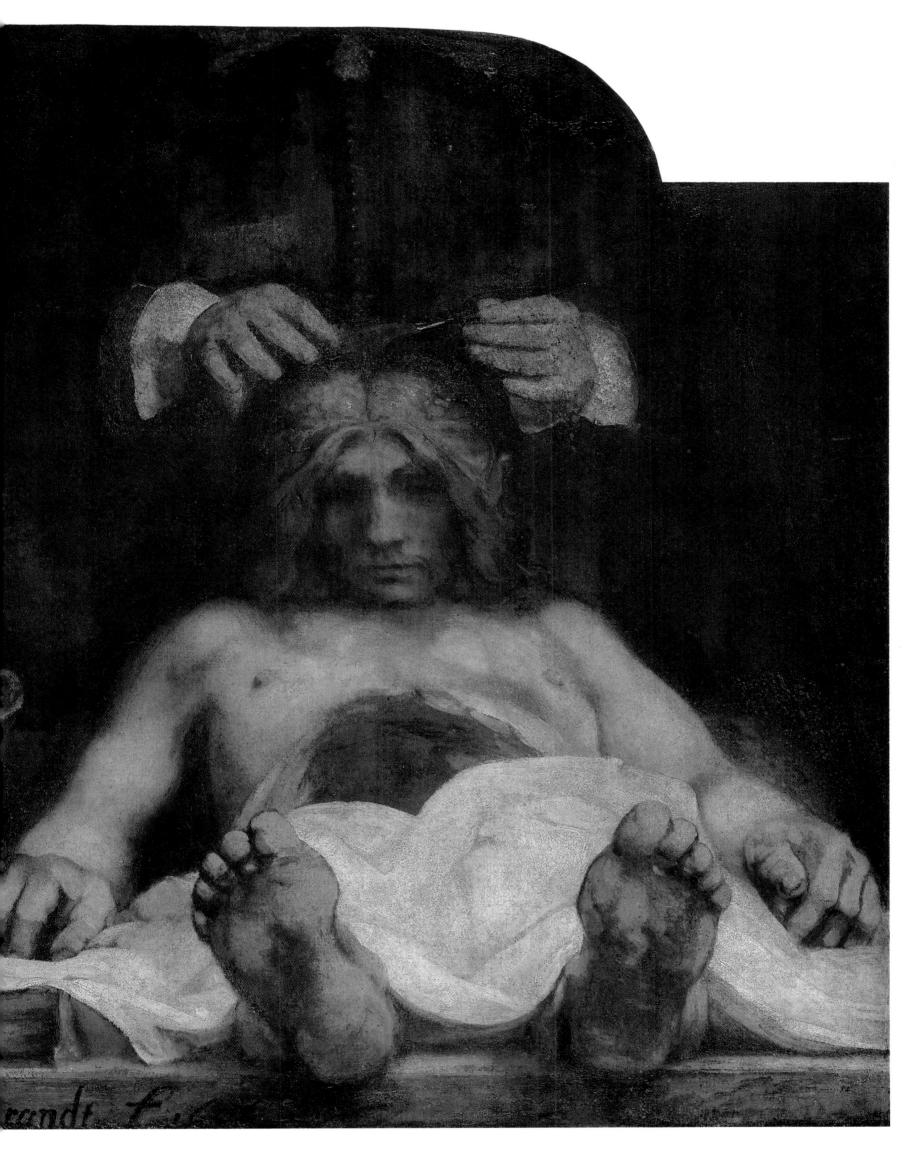

JACOB BLESSING THE SONS OF JOSEPH, 1656
Oil on canvas,
68½ × 82¼ inches (175.5 × 210.5 cm)
Gemäldegalerie, Kassel

Above:
JUNO, *c.* 1661
Oil on canvas,
49½ × 42 inches (127 × 107.5 cm)
Armand Hammer Foundation, Los Angeles

Right:
JACOB TRIP, 1661
Oil on canvas,
51 × 37⅞ inches (130.5 × 97 cm)
The National Gallery, London

Left:
SELF-PORTRAIT, 1660
Oil on canvas,
43¼ × 33¼ inches (111 × 8.5 cm)
Musée du Louvre, Paris

Above:
SELF-PORTRAIT, *c.*1661-62
Oil on canvas,
44⅝ × 37⅛ inches (114.3 × 95.2 cm)
The Iveagh Bequest, Kenwood House, London

THE CONSPIRACY OF CLAUDIUS CIVILIUS,
1661-62
Oil on canvas,
76½ × 120¾ inches (196 × 309 cm)
Nationalmuseum, Stockholm

'THE JEWISH BRIDE,' *c.*1662
Oil on canvas,
47½ × 65 inches (121.5 × 166.5 cm)
Rijksmuseum, Amsterdam

THE SAMPLING OFFICIALS OF THE DRAPERS'
GUILD (THE SYNDICS), 1662
Oil on canvas,
74¾ × 109 inches (191.5 × 279 cm)
Rijksmuseum, Amsterdam

A FAMILY GROUP, *c.*1663-68
Oil on canvas,
49¼ × 65¼ inches (126 × 167 cm)
Herzog Anton Ulrich-Museum, Braunschweig

SELF-PORTRAIT, 1669
Oil on canvas,
33½ × 27½ inches (86 × 70.5 cm)
The National Gallery, London

Self-Portrait, 1669
Oil on canvas,
24¾ × 22½ inches (63.5 × 57.8 cm)
The Mauritshuis, The Hague

Acknowledgments

The publisher would like to thank Martin Bristow for designing this book. We should also like to thank the following institutions, individuals and agencies for permission to reproduce photographic material.

Alte Pinakothek, Munich/Artothek: pages 44, 45, 50

Armand Hammer Foundation, Los Angeles: page 98

Courtesy of the Trustees of the British Museum, London: pages 1, 12, 16, 19, 21, 48

Collection of the Duke of Buccleuch, Drumlanrig Castle, Scotland: page 88

Dulwich Picture Gallery, London: page 72

The Frick Collection, New York: pages 13, 96

Isabella Stewart Gardner Museum, Boston: page 46

Gemäldegalerie, Dresden: page 57

Gemäldegalerie, Kassel: pages 63, 73, 74-75, 94-95

Gemäldegalerie, Museen Preussischen Kulturbesitz, Berlin: pages 14, 24-25, 52, 78-79, 91

J Paul Getty Museum, Malibu: page 38

Glasgow Museums; Art Gallery and Museum, Kelvingrove: page 87

Hermitage Museum, St Petersburg: page 55

Herzog Anton Ulrich Museum, Braunschweig: pages 108-109

Historisches Museum, Amsterdam: page 7

Hunterian Museum and Art Gallery, Glasgow: page 65

The Iveagh Bequest, Kenwood House, London: page 101

Kunsthistorisches Museum, Vienna: page 9, 90

The Mauritshuis, The Hague: pages 29, 37, 111

Metropolitan Museum of Art, New York: page 39 (Bequest of William Kijk Vanderbilt, 1920), 80-81 (Purchased with Special Funds and Gifts of Friends of the Museum, 1961), 83 (Gift of Archer M Huntington in memory of his father Collis Potter Huntington)

Musée des Beaux-Arts, Lyon: page 22

Musée Jacquemart-André, Paris: pages 26-27

Musée du Louvre, Paris, photo RMN: pages 6, 18, 64, 85-85, 100

Museum Boymans-van Beuningen, Rotterdam: page 89

Museum of Fine Arts, Boston: pages 30-31

Museum het Rembrandthuis, Amsterdam: page 11

Courtesy of the Trustees of the National Gallery, London: pages 2, 15, 47, 49, 53, 54, 56, 60-61, 62, 68, 76, 77, 82, 99, 110

Nationalmuseum, Stockholm: pages 102-103

Private Collection: pages 32-33

Rijksmuseum, Amsterdam: pages 17, 23, 28, 35, 36, 40-41, 66, 67, 70-71 (on loan from the City of Amsterdam), 92-93 (on loan from the City of Amsterdam), 97, 104-105, 106-107

Royal Collection, Buckingham Palace © 1994 Her Majesty the Queen: pages 42-43, 51, 69

Royal Collection, Windsor Castle © 1994 Her Majesty the Queen: page 34

Six Collection, Amsterdam: page 86

Staatliche Graphische Sammlung, Munich: page 20

Städelsches Kunstinstitut, Frankfurt: pages 58-59

Stedelijk Museum de Lakenhal, Leiden: page 10